Loads of Cartoons!

A compendium of gags from UK cartoonist Nigel Sutherland

These cartoons are just a small selection from the thousands of gags I have produced over the years.

In the UK, I've appeared in a variety of publications, most commonly The Sun newspaper, whilst abroad, I've been published in countries as diverse as Italy, the USA, and China.

Although the cartoons within this collection are in no particular order, it may be quite easy to distinguish between those produced in my early cartooning years, and those that are more recent. During an enjoyable journey, my style has certainly evolved.

I hope you find something within these pages to make you smile!

Nigel Sutherland

Dedicated to my late father, Brian Sutherland, who I thank for giving me a sense of humour, as well as any artistic ability I may possess.

First Published by Nigel Sutherland 2009
www.nigelsutherland.co.uk

ISBN 978-1-4092-5694-6

Design and layout by Tartan Design, Rothesay, Scotland, UK.

"Now you know why I cross the road."

"If your chef's that good, how come he's never been on the telly?"

“We sold all OUR junk. He bought this new junk off the table next door.”

"As this is a civil ceremony, I'd rather you took the vows without swearing."

"You know nothing about auctions, antiques, cookery, or house-buying, yet you expect to work in television?"

"We've an appointment with Merlin."

"He acts the clown too much for my liking."

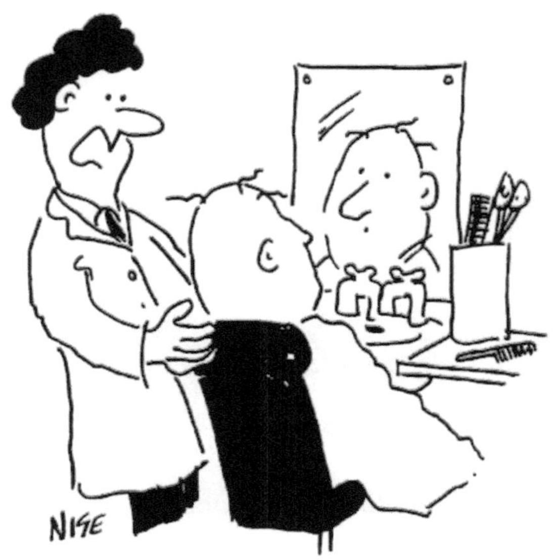

"Well, sir - shall I plait 'em, count 'em, or shall we just make do with a polish?"

"I'm sure there's a page that tells you how to paper around awkward objects."

"Hands up the table with the underdone lobster."

"On TV they play dramatic music as the contestants enter the ring."

"See what I mean about being awkward?"

"Just how far do these Best-Man duties extend?"

"This bill's not a pretty sight either"

"No-one else would brag about being on 'Rogue Traders'."

"Other bird-fanciers' little pets don't work behind the bar of The Red Lion."

"There are times I worry about him - he could do himself a nasty injury with that bottle-opener."

"Okay - let's forget the budget treatment."

"Undamaged, it would have been worth a small fortune."

"Certain of you may already have your hearts set on what you want to be in life."

"Tell the sign company we want that B replacing as a matter of urgency."

"I quite agree - the weather has been pretty dreadful lately."

"What's so special about seeing a horse box?"

"They've certainly got some pretty quaint place names in the part of the world."

"At least the mess I make is all in one place."

"We've had a cash-machine put in."

"When you said, 'See ewe in my office'..."

"Look, is it 'Buy one, get one free',
or 'Two for the price of one'?"

"Can I ask the audience?"

"What have you got for someone
I don't like very much?"

"Yes, 'he does', - next question..."

"He only has a chaser when his wife finds him with a girlfriend."

CARAVAN
CLUB SHOP
HOSIERY
HOLD
-UPS
NISE

RED
LION
HAPPY
HOUR
6-7
NISE

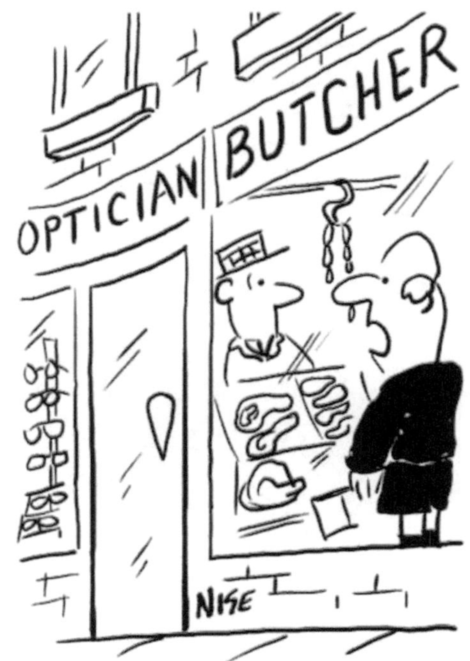

"Could you give me an eye-test before the new football season starts?"

"He's gone on a lap-of-honour!"

"My wife loves doing puzzles - she cooked me three last week."

"Well, it may appear sound, Mr Pig, but in my opinion, a huff or a puff could soon bring the place down."

"I'm spending our Home Improvement Grant on a leaving party for you."

"I haven't a clue who he is - must be a 'celebrity'."

"Would you like me to take 'Mr & Mrs Smith' as your final answer?"

"Threatening to call the Noise Abatement Society isn't being very romantic, Sydney."

"I've invented some new gossip
I'd like circulating."

"Funny how the pub quiz champion
can't tell what time it is."

"That reminds me - it's time
I dumped the boyfriend."

"I understand your perfumes are pretty effective."

"I can get a bottle from the Off Licence that'd improve your looks."

"Two chicken burgers and a portion of fries, please."

"You've been matched with a pub in Ramsgate."

"Sir wants something more than simply 'two, both blue', Norman."

"I blame his old careers teacher myself - it was he who suggested a bank job."

"I'd say you were in perfect shape - that's if you were a Sumo wrestler."

"George reckons he's getting the hang of shopping over the internet."

"I'm looking for a 'stay-at-home' type, so I can go drinking in peace."

"Look, I paid the cash - you can do the carrying."

"Yes, I know we ordered 'breakfast in bed', but..."

"We're having another leadership contest."

"How thoughtful, dear - a new iron to match my set of saucepans."

"It's six letters, and the third one's 'e'."

"To him, on-line dating's chatting up women on the train home."

"When I said 'Show her a loving husband', Mr Jones, I didn't mean a picture of your friend, Wally."

"What's in the cauldron today, dear?"

"Look, can't you take it in turns
to do the daily Sudoku?"

"You didn't have to tell them I 'walk the streets' - I'm not ashamed to be a Traffic Warden."

"Might that be where the tooth is hurting, Mr Lloyd?"

"The shock to my system could be detrimental."

"Oh yes... and I'll want one for the wife as well."

"Is this the Lonely Hearts Club?"

"Of course you're very dear to me
- that meal just cost a fortune."

"Dear customers - we are pleased to announce that in five minutes, everything in the store will be drastically reduced."

"Okay - I'll enter "beauty queen", "millionairess", and "pub landlady" and we'll see what comes up."

"I'll say one thing about this pub - you do get a better class of riff-raff."

"Eric won't watch 'The Budget'
in case it taxes his brain."

"Look - it's the managerial merry-go-round."

"Well, here's your final pub quiz question, 'Whose is the blonde hair on your jacket?'"

"Any chance of a Ploughman's?"

"Do you have to say 'cheese' every time we pass a speed camera?"

"I never help washing-up? Once again she conveniently forgets June 3rd, 1987."

"Then I foolishly said, 'I don't want to see you lazing around all day'."

"So then the Relate counsellor said, 'Try putting yourself in his place for a while'."

"You're right, they have spelt 'Printed in China' incorrectly."

"I didn't report him missing, so why should I have him back?"

"I couldn't give up the fags, so I've started drinking long-life milk instead."

"He is romantic in his own way - I mean he's out celebrating our wedding anniversary as I speak."

"You will shortly be losing a lot of money. That'll be £50 please."

"How do you get rid of them once they're attracted?"

"I'm in for something I didn't do
- I didn't arrange a getaway car."

"One with rose-coloured spectacles
might be good."

"I'm a rock climber - I know how challenging a craggy face can be."

"No we're not there yet - Daddy has to reverse off the drive first."

"Nothing against naturist holidays, Sir,
- it's just that we'd rather you kept your
clothes on 'til you actually got there."

"Please put the ring on her finger,
Mr Stroodle. I'm sure she'll give
you a receipt after the service."

"Stick to webs, son - we don't do woolly jumpers."

"All is safely gathered in."

"Look mate - a dream holiday for two wouldn't include him."

"I'd like to go to the one most deserving."

"For our second honeymoon to be better than the first, he'd have to stay at home."

"It definitely said, 'After cooking, stand for two minutes'."

"Hello, you're through to our special help lion."

"I told you you'd got Jimmy's homework wrong."

"Quick, make something up - I've got a space to fill."

"Dream dates don't normally go for nightmares."

"Look, it definitely says on the sign that we're over there."

"I'm a football referee - I'll have a box of red and a box of yellow."

"A man in uniform? Well, we've two park keepers, six traffic wardens, and a deckchair attendant."

“Okay, Mr Johnston, open your eyes!”

“Hi - I’m on the train right now...”

"Your 'walking-bus' to the pub's arrived."

"He used to be my heart-throb, now he just gives me palpitations."

"Do we have to have that sign on there every time we take Mother shopping?"

"Oh he's sporty all right - he can be up and down on his stairlift in under ten minutes."

"Do YOU think solitude drives you crazy?"

"I personally feel you could be more selective in your choice, Mr Jones."

"Have you checked your E-I-E-I-O mail?"

"Of course we can't 'share a suitcase'.
Not if I'm in Greece and he's in Margate."

"Which side of the road would you like me to drive on today?"

"I'm sorry, but shouldn't there be an apostrophe in that?"

"Perhaps you can have the chair by the window next week, Mr Jones."

"Something for the 'week' end, Sir?"

"What's the damage?"

"No we don't sell gin and tonic."

"I wouldn't say he gets NO exercise - he does have to use his thumbs on the remote."

"It's definitely grown hyacinth
we last looked at it."

"Nothing romantic or lovey-dovey,
it's for the wife."

"Okay if I enter the disaster area, dear?"

"You're deliberately agreeing with me
to make me look foolish."

"And there'd be no extra charge for keeping me out late, trying to persuade you."

"The path of Love Street's always gone downhill."

"Yes, I once swore my love for him - now I just swear at him."

"The policeman's been replaced by a traffic-warden with extended powers."

"Half the time we get on fine, the other half, he's here."

"You're going to school, and that's final. I'm sure other Head-Teachers don't play up like this."

"Must be for this new-fangled 'email'."

"So, on the face of it, what's your verdict?"

"Well, would it be okay if I just did some putting?"

"And your pudding stays clamped 'til
you've eaten all your vegetables."

"They lost again - I'm changing
my allegiance!"

"This one, we're training to work on the railways."

"Right, Sir, so that's one lottery ticket, both draws, for the next five weeks."

"I smell spring in the air. Let's take the caravan out and hold up some traffic!"

"Well they're certainly overworking these doctors - I only got up to use the lavatory."

"It's not the kind of night club I was hoping you'd be taking me to, Doreen."

"Look, do you want rescuing, or not?"

"I think we need to discuss your bedside manner, Doctor Jenkins."

"You'll never be a member of the 'idle rich', but at least you're halfway there..."

"Ah, Reception? It's about this 'sea-view' I was promised..."

"Could you broaden your choice? There's not much call for lighthouse-keepers in Wigan."

"It's a pity his favourite soaps don't include the one in the bathroom."

"He said we'd 'push the boat out' for my birthday, then took me down the lifeboat station."

"The 'wrong change'? But... It can't be... Say it's not true! Please, please... Oh, woe is me!"

"His 'get-up-and-go', got up and went, years ago!"

"You could at least try and look a bit like Alan Titchmarsh."

"It's the happiest day of MY life, son
- I just let your old bedroom."

"Once more, from the top..."

"I'll check again but I'm pretty sure 'drinking all day' isn't one of the activities."

"Climate-change only seems to affect us when we come away on holiday."

"There isn't really time for your lawyers to go over the small print, Mr Johnson."

"Shall I save a sole for you, Vicar?"

"We've had a rush of people looking
for affordable housing."

www.ingramcontent.com/pod-product-compliance
Ingram Content Group UK Ltd.
Pitfield, Milton Keynes, MK11 3LW, UK
UKHW041932190726
13854UKWH00004B/1554